HOW TO GET THAT JOB: THE SIMPLE AND COMPREHENSIVE GUIDE TO A SUCCESSFUL INTERVIEW

Sara T Patrick

Copyright

Table of Contents

CHAPTER ONE: What sets you apart?

Asking what sets you apart from other candidates during an interview is a vital approach for hiring managers to differentiate you from other applicants. Employers are seeking people who can provide the most value to their organization. By evaluating how you can contribute to a certain function, this question acts as an opportunity to clarify your skill set, display your confidence and be as prepared as possible for your interview

Hiring managers prefer to ask interview questions such as, “what makes you unique?” or, “what sets you apart from other candidates?”

They use this to test your confidence, but also to determine how well you understand the position you’re interviewing for. Specifically, companies use this question to give you a chance to elaborate upon your special talents, drives, ambitions, strengths, and relevant experience whilst applying them to this employment opportunity. They're urging you to acknowledge your talents and best traits with confidence and to describe why your skills and qualifications make you the greatest applicant for the post.

They also ask this question to evaluate if you've researched the role and company. This question is an excellent approach for employers to judge how much you know about the position and institution. Researching the role in detail allows you to examine the particular attributes that may make you a great candidate. It also provides an opportunity for hiring managers to examine how much preparation and ingenuity you've put into preparing for your interview.

And there are a handful of ideas you NEED to keep in mind if you want to differ from other applicants and get the job offer.

1. Always do your research

The first thing you need to do before heading for that interview is to make sure you understand the role. Study the job description as a part of your pre-interview study.

If you're not investigating the company… recruiters and hiring managers can tell. And they're going to hire someone who's put in the extra effort to learn about the position before coming in to interview.

So don't skip this.

2. Relate your background to the position's needs – and include anything distinctive about you

This suggestion is vital if you are submitting a cover letter ahead of the interview. Once you've done your homework, the following step is to point out the most relevant elements of your background in your cover letter. What have you done that's most similar to what the organization needs in its job? That's how to impress while answering this question (as well as queries such, "Why should we hire you?")

So for example, you may say:

"I noted on the job description that you're seeking someone who can conduct a mix of data entry and data analysis. One piece of experience that sets me apart from other candidates is my expert-level mastery of Excel. In my former work, I was responsible for developing many pivot tables each month to assist us to evaluate complex data, so I think I'd have a distinct advantage in this role and would be able to offer more than other candidates."

Always try to compare your background to the work and their needs.

3:Focus on your most prized assets

This question is an opportunity for you to stand out, so think about those traits that make you distinctive and can potentially provide value to the firm. Making these logical connections between your skill set and the role itself will help you feel prepared and confident. By exhibiting confidence in yourself throughout the interview, you inspire a sense of assuredness in the interviewer that you're a good candidate for the post.

4: Keep your answer relevant: Make sure to stay on topic while discussing your answer. Although you may want to discuss all of your skills and experience, only discuss which ones apply to the role. This can help your answer stay focused and concise.

5:Figure out what makes you special: Although discussing your relevant skills is helpful, you need to figure out why you stand out among all of the other candidates. Elaborate on a special talent or unique experience you have. Think about what other people might say and how you can make your answer different.

6:Share past examples: Talking about particular occasions you brought value to your team might help you showcase what makes you distinctive. Think about a period when you were the only person who was able to solve a problem.

7:Be confident and polite: Although you should indicate that you are confident about your response, you should also be aware of how you talk to other applicants. Find a balance between sharing your gifts and speaking graciously of others. There is no need to badmouth other candidates to illustrate your case.

CHAPTER TWO: "Tell me about yourself" why this question pops up often

Tell me about yourself" could seem like an easy win of an interview question—after all, you know everything about yourself! And good thing, too, because it's often the first thing an interviewer will ask you to do—whether you're having a preliminary phone screen, speaking to your prospective boss, or sitting down with the CEO during the final round.

But responding to this offer to communicate about yourself in the context of a job interview can feel uncomfortable and complex. You could be thinking: Um, what do you want to know? Should I offer you the full narrative of my workplace drama complete with ideal casting? You should prepare in advance so you can use this typical opening prompt to your advantage, setting the stage for a successful interview.

As with every interview question, the key to producing an impressive answer is understanding why people are asking in the first place. This question is a wonderful starting point that can assist inform the path of the interview. What you say helps them figure out the next question which may help create a chain effect of follow-up questions, offer an easy flow to the conversation, and allow recruiters and hiring managers to accomplish one of their primary goals in the hiring process: getting to know you.

If you answer it correctly, the interviewers will begin to find out why you're the greatest candidate for this job, in terms of hard abilities and experience as well as soft talents. It's a terrific opportunity to demonstrate that you can speak clearly and successfully, connect with and react to other humans, and present yourself professionally.

There are plenty of situations when you'll hear these same words: "Tell me about yourself." But interviewers might have different interpretations of the prompt that are asking pretty much the same thing, including:

I have your resume in front of me but tell me more about yourself.
Walk me through your resume.
I'd love to hear more about your trip.
Tell me a little bit more about your background.

You have to understand that the interviewers want to know more about you so that you would not be caught off guard when asked this question.

Dos and don'ts when answering “tell me about yourself” in an interview

To summarise, here is a list of ways to answer this typical interview question as well as issues to consider avoiding.

DO's \sConnect personal strengths to supporting instances.
Keep your response to two minutes or less.
Focus on details and outcomes you can quantify.
Speak about what sets you distinct from other contenders.
Mention past experiences and demonstrated accomplishments.
Align your present job tasks to the role.
Avoid mentioning personal details about your marital status, children, and political or religious opinions.
Highlight your personality.
Avoid rushing into deeper conversations about the role and company.

Connect your abilities to the job description.

Briefly discuss interests, intellectual development, and community involvement.

Write down an example answer and practice.

DON'Ts

Mention highly personal details such as marital status, children, political or religious affiliations, etc. These can be sensitive topics that might work against you as a candidate, not to mention such facts should not be factors for the employer in judging your capacity to perform the job.

List many, ambiguous strengths without supporting examples. Instead, you may wish to choose two or three attributes about yourself. Support each with brief, polished stories that can be substantiated by your job experience.

Memorize your response. While it's helpful to practice and memorize your major points, you don't want to memorize your answer word for word since it has the potential to come off as robotic and unnatural.

Summarize your resume word for word. Instead, discuss high points that are relevant to the position.

Rush into conversations regarding what you're looking for in the role or how the company may benefit you—save such subjects for the later stages of the interview process when they are sold on you as a candidate and you have more influence.

HOW TO ANSWER "TELL ME ABOUT YOURSELF"

Begin with a brief explanation of where you are currently (which could include your present employment combined with a mention of a personal pastime or passion) (which could include your current job along with a reference to a personal hobby or passion)

Reference how you got to where you are (here you might cite school, or a key experience such as a former job, internship, or volunteer activity) (here you could mention education, or an important experience such as a past job, internship, or volunteer experience)

Finish by touching on a goal for the future.

Every good answer to “tell me about yourself” should consist of:

Work - This should make up roughly 80% of your answer. Focus on your previous experience and accomplishments here.

Academic - 10-15% of your answer should then be about your academic background (university, academic achievements, etc). (university, academic achievements, etc.).

Personal - Finally the last 5-10% should be about you as a person, while still keeping it relevant to the company.

I would recommend utilizing this format while addressing the question

The history - what is your background and relevant work experience? How did you get to where you are now?
The present - what is your current role? What do you do and what are your biggest accomplishments?
The future - what are you looking to do next? Why are you interested in the position?

Keeping these guidelines in mind, here's what a decent answer to "tell me about yourself" would look like:

Correct Answer:\s“Sure, well, my name is Zoe and I am 24 years old.

For the past 5 years, I’ve been working as a business analyst for companies A and B.

I have some background in data analysis, having a degree from University XY. What got me into the sector, though, is the internship I performed at Company C.

Throughout my work, I’ve observed that I’ve always been adept with statistics and handling data.

For example, when I was working at Company X, I oversaw a project for moving all operations data to a new data warehousing system to cut down on costs. The new system was a far better fit for our firm, which finally led to savings of up to $20,000 yearly.

Moving forward, I wish to expand my experience across numerous industries. Particularly fintech, which is why I'm interested in your company.."

Here's what's done right:

The answer is personalized. Zoe doesn't veer off-topic, she talks about her experience as a business analyst and his former triumphs in working with data.
The answer is based on experiences and achievements. Zoe talks about her work experience as a business analyst and covers some of her top achievements.
The answer is organized appropriately - past, present, future.
Sounds simple enough, right?

Awesome!

3 TELL ME ABOUT YOURSELF SAMPLE ANSWERS

Need some inspiration? Here are 3 sample answers:

Experienced professionals
Fresh graduates and college students
University admissions
Ready? Let's start with:

Sample Answer for Experienced Professionals:

Sure, I'd be pleased to. I've been a tech-focused project manager for up to 6 years now.

I graduated from University X, where I earned the Dean's List, with a degree in business administration and a minor in computer science. After that, I initially got into the sector by working as an administrative assistant at Company X. There I offered clerical support with interdepartmental communication, aided in organizing schedules, and maintained the digital filing system.

After that, I was working as a project manager for Company Y which supplied cloud computing solutions for nearly 4 years. There, I team on software projects and made sure everything ran well in terms of business goals, deadlines, money, and more.

In my downtime, I enjoy reading about AI, tech, and robotics. Since you guys do all 3, I figured I'd apply.

Sample Answer for Fresh Graduates and College Students:

My name is Sandra, I'm 22 years old and I recently graduated from University X with a B.A. in international business. While there, I learned a lot of theories in subjects like corporate communication, international economics, corporate governance, and more. I was also a member of the student government and maintained a GPA of 3.6.

I’ve worked hard in my study and now I’m ready to apply my knowledge to practice.

While I don’t have any real-life work experience, I’ve had a lot of exposure to the corporate environment. A lot of my courses entailed working with real companies to solve real challenges.

Now, I’m looking to leverage everything I’ve learned in uni and get some hands-on work experience.

Sample Answer for University Admissions:

So, my name is John, and I’m a senior at School XYZ.

This year, I managed to maintain a 3.7 GPA, while working on a few different school projects. I started a 'Rapid talent Book Club' which has up to 20 active members as of now. And I also launched a recycling program for the campus, through which we raised awareness and invited an outside guest lecturer to speak about the subject.

I tend to be teamwork-oriented and reliable, as I've never missed a deadline. I'm also proud of my ability to preserve and overcome any challenges as they come up. For example, last year, I was having some problems with trigonometry. I realized I needed to dedicate more time to the subject, so, I met with a teacher outside the class and set aside two extra hours per day for the subject. Eventually, I ended up with an A on the topic.

At University X, I'm planning to either major in English or Journalism. I love reading and writing, so I think both programs are going to be intriguing and related to my interests.

CHAPTER THREE: PRACTICING AHEAD OF THE INTERVIEW

Taking the time to practice for a job interview will make you feel more comfortable during the job interview, enhance your interview skills, and raise your chances of earning a job offer.

What's the greatest approach to practice?

Rehearsing is one of the finest strategies to prepare for a job interview. You can practice with a professional, ask a family member or friend to help out, or practice by yourself. A mock interview with a professional is one technique to acquire and practice interviewing skills, as well as using an online interview preparation tool. Depending on the services you utilize, these may be fee-based possibilities, but you can still practice even if you can't afford expert guidance.

Advantages of honing your interview skills

1. Reduce stress and anxiety

For the majority of people, the interview process is a dreaded, high-pressure, anxiety-riddled affair. Unfortunately, not only is that exceedingly painful, but it can also significantly influence your performance. All too often, nervousness and stress during an interview can make it impossible to recall your experiences and maintain a healthy two-way interaction. A practice interview allows you to acquaint yourself with the interview atmosphere in a low-stress environment, giving you time to learn how to best manage your anxieties and lessen some of the tension associated with feeling underprepared. It also allows chatting with an interview specialist about nerve-calming tactics that you can apply for your future interview.

2. Boost your confidence

When it comes to interviewing, confidence is crucial. Even the most qualified candidate may be overlooked if their personality and expertise do not come through during the interview; after all, you have to believe in yourself for others to believe in you. By enabling you to practice responding to new questions, identifying what you can do better before the interview, and leading you to strengthen your overall performance, a practice interview can give you greater assurance in your capabilities. Going through the process of interviewing – even if it does not count – will help ensure that you are well prepared for your real interview, and in so doing, you'll feel more confident in your ability to do well.

3. Learn techniques to help you answer unanticipated questions

Anyone can rehearse answers to a set of questions, but one tricky aspect of most interviews is that the interviewee does not know in advance which questions they will be asked. A benefit of practice interviews is that the majority of the appointment is focused on giving personalized feedback on how to answer specific types of questions, rather than on how to answer only those asked in the mock interview. During your appointment, the interview specialist will go over the general categories of questions that are asked in interviews, explaining what is being assessed through each and how to best structure your response. Being aware of what to look for will help you identify the best way to answer even the most unanticipated question when it is time for the real interview.

These questions can be particularly tricky because many of them require personalized responses, and therefore cannot necessarily be answered through a quick Google search. One of the greatest benefits of a practice interview is that you can ask those lingering questions and be certain that the individual responding is giving you an answer that is not only grounded in expertise but also tailored to your specific concern.

From reducing nerves and boosting your confidence, to giving you personalized advice and equipping you to pursue your professional goals, practice interviews have been found to have several significant benefits.

At the end of the day, practice makes perfect; and what better way to practice interviewing than through a practice interview?

CHAPTER FOUR: HOW TO ANSWER COMMON AND PERSONALIZED QUESTIONS(WHY SHOULD WE HIRE YOU, DO YOU HAVE ANY QUESTIONS FOR US)

Employers want to make sure you know what they want and that you can offer it. They have a hunch you're qualified enough to get the job done. That's why they're inviting you for a face-to-face interview. They want to make sure you understand what they do and that you're a cultural match. Here's the thing: others are likewise qualified, perhaps more than you. You must use your interview to get your company to recognize that you are the one who will best fit.

So, use the why should I hire you? question to sell them yourself once and for all.

How to Answer Why Should We Hire You

1. Show that you have the expertise and experience to execute the job and generate exceptional results.

You never know what other candidates offer to the firm. But you know you: stress your essential qualities, strengths, talents, job experience, and professional successes that are fundamental to getting amazing things done in this role.

2. Highlight that you'll fit in and be a terrific asset to the team.

Show the interviewer that you have corresponding personal and professional attributes that make you a fantastic asset to the organization. At larger companies, departments and their workforce vary substantially. Marketing folks are distinct from IT specialists. Identify the company's culture and the department's characteristic qualities and tell the interviewer how you will fit in.

3. Describe how hiring you will make their life easier and help them achieve more.

Determine what challenges they had so far, what new issues or goals they have now, and how your special abilities and experience can come in handy. Scour the company's website and social media channels to understand its roadmap and history. Google their media mentions and case studies. Reread the job post you applied to. Use this information to guide your answer.

4. Show excitement for executing essential duties, not simply capability.

Your application lets them know you're willing to do the work. Being called for the interview shows they think you're capable. Apart from displaying your talents and expertise, show them your passion to ensure you'll have a good attitude towards your tasks. But don't go overboard—a big smile can never substitute professional qualifications.

5. Always talk honestly.

Be honest with both yourself and your prospective employer. You won't make it far if you lie. Recruiters often ask follow-up questions to see if you're consistent with what you've said on your résumé.

Sample Answer To "why Should We Hire You?"

"I know it's been an exciting period for General Tech—growing so much and acquiring multiple startups—but I also know from experience that it may be tough for the sales staff to comprehend how new products fit in with the old ones. It's often simpler to market the product you know, so the newest stuff can get shortchanged, which can have company-wide repercussions. I have almost a decade of experience as a sales trainer, but more significantly, most of those years were dealing with sales teams that were in the same scenario Gen Tech is in now. Growth is excellent, but only if the rest of the firm can keep up. I'm convinced I can make sure your sales force is confident and passionate about selling new items by establishing an ongoing sales training curriculum that stresses where they place in a product lineup."

How to Respond To "Do You Have Any Questions for Me?"

As an interview draws to a close, the interviewer may typically ask, "Do you have any questions for me?"

Even though coming up with inquiries can be tough, it's always preferable to react with a question than to respectfully decline. Otherwise, you could leave interviewers with the sense that you're not engaged with the talk, or that you're not interested enough in the position to jump at the opportunity to learn more.

In some ways, there's a pretty obvious reason for interviewers to ask if you have any questions: They want to allow you to get answers to queries that may help you decide if the role and organization are a good fit for you.

Plus, since it's such a popular end to interviews, this question allows employers to determine if you prepared in advance.

Your questions should make it evident that you were engaged during the interview and have rapidly gained a sense of the company's aims and priorities. You might reflect on earlier points in the interview or build off news within the firm or its market. And keep in mind, like with all interview questions, this one allows you to wow. By asking a meaningful, solid question, you can close out the interview by providing the interviewers with a good impression. Plus, interviews are a two-way street, and asking questions can be a fantastic method to discover if the organization and role at hand are a suitable fit for you. If you find it hard getting a question, Ask wherever question you would have asked if you started work instantly.

CHAPTER FIVE: 20 Common Interview Questions You Can Use For Your Practice Interview

I do advocate spending some time getting acquainted with what you might be asked, what hiring managers are truly looking for in your responses, and what it takes to show that you're the perfect person for the job.

Consider this list as your interview question and answer study guide.

How did you hear about this position?
Why do you want to work at this company?
What are your biggest strengths?
What do you perceive to be your weaknesses?

Tell me about a challenge or dispute you've had at work, and how you dealt with it

Tell me about a time you made a mistake.

Tell me about a time you displayed leadership qualities.

Why are you quitting your current job?

What are you searching for in a new position?

How do you deal with pressure or difficult situations?

What do you prefer to do outside of work?

How do you prioritize your work?

What are you enthusiastic about?

How do you like to be managed?

How do you plan to reach your career goals?

What makes you unique?

What are your pay expectations?

When can you start?

Describe your dream job.

What can we expect from you in your first three months?

CHAPTER SIX: The Right Way to Carry Yourself And Look Confident

If you have a job interview coming up, it's only normal to be worried, especially if you don't have a lot of experience in the industry. But one of the most critical aspects of every interview is confidence. If you can create and transmit self-confidence, you'll be shocked at how far it can carry you. Here's what you should know.

WHY CONFIDENCE MATTERS

Put yourself in your interviewer's shoes for a second. The company is counting on you to employ someone who can step straight in and do the job, work well with the team, take direction and make the workplace a little better overall. You interview two applicants with equal backgrounds and experience. One is confident and comforting, whereas the other is apprehensive and dubious of her ability. Which one makes you feel confident that she can accomplish the job? In other words, why should the interviewer trust in you if you don't believe in yourself?

Confidence counts since it shows that you trust your ability. You know you can perform the job, and you know you will be an asset to the firm. Specific talents can be taught, but you have to prove that you can learn and use them.

HOW TO BUILD YOUR CONFIDENCE BEFORE AN INTERVIEW

Of all, you can't merely click your fingers and suddenly become more confident. But there are a few tips you can follow:

Prepare yourself: It's always useful to investigate the company and its role. But beyond that, study what you can about the interview process itself. Who will interview you? What's the format? Where is the meeting room? Just knowing what to expect might minimize your nerves and make you feel more confident.

Remember your strengths: The interviewer wants to know what value you provide to the firm. So before your interview, identify a few things you've done that make you proud. Maybe you successfully negotiated a tough scenario or completed a goal. Whatever those things are, be ready to talk about them in your interview.

Interview the interviewer: Don't be scared to modify the relationship between yourself and the interviewer. You need to determine whether the employee is suited for you. Asking questions and analyzing whether it's the appropriate fit can help you feel like an active part of the process, which in turn can enhance your confidence.

5 strategies to look confident during an interview

1. Just Breathe

While waiting to be greeted by your interviewer, take a few moments to do some breathing. (Yes, like a pregnant woman in labor!) By doing this, you may shift the difficult emotion you're experiencing (e.g., worry or fear) and be able to focus on something else (in this example, the fantastic job that you're expecting to land). Holistic health specialist Andrew Weil, MD promotes breathing exercises, saying, “Since breathing is something we can control and regulate, it is a great tool for creating a relaxed and clear frame of mind.”

To do this most efficiently, take a deep breath through your nose (really feel your tummy expand) and then gently blow it out through your mouth. Repeat this three times, while focussing on centering your mind. The wonderful thing about this approach is that you can do it anywhere (and fairly unnoticeably), so if you feel your nerves start to swell during the interview, simply take another breath.

2. Don’t Fidget

Nervous fidgeting is one of the most unmistakable signals that you’re nervous, thus this is an immensely vital habit to acquire. My go-to tactic is to keep my hands clasped together on the table or in my lap to avoid any subconscious table tapping, hair twirling, or otherwise noticeable wriggling. I'm also a leg-shaker—but keeping my hands in my lap and providing a bit of pressure on my legs helps remind me to limit the shaking to a minimum.

If you think you don't have any fidgety behaviors, you might want to think again—most individuals aren't conscious of their nervous tendencies because they're such an embedded part of their normal behavior. To double-check, try doing a few mock interviews with a buddy who can call you out on any fidgeting. Once you know exactly what to avoid, you may practice controlling it.

3. Make Eye Contact

One of the best ways to deceive a hiring manager into thinking you're more confident than you feel is to keep consistent, natural eye contact throughout the interview. Mary Griffin, a Human Resources Director for a national healthcare organization says, "A big giveaway of a nervous Nellie is a lack of direct eye contact—looking down, looking away, and not facing the interviewer straight in the eyes. A more confident interviewee appears to be engaged with the interviewer."

One approach to remind oneself to make regular eye contact is to focus on a location between the interviewer's eyes. You can even visualize a colorful bulls-eye there—whatever it takes to keep your eyes from wandering too much.

On the flip hand, you don't want to be so totally focused on making eye contact that you wind up sending out a weird vibe! So remember to take natural breaks, like gazing down at your CV every once in a while. It's a balancing act, so simply keep practicing until it feels comfortable.

4. Press Pause

Some of us (myself included!) tend to babble when we're scared. This can be problematic because once we start talking, it's quite simple to go off subject and say more than what's needed—or worse, more than what's suitable.

To prevent any rambling, I attempt to answer each question with only one concept or idea at a time. For example, if you're asked to describe a feature you disliked about a past supervisor, you may respond, "I found that her tendency to micromanage contrasted with my productivity." Then stop. This will spare you from unneeded add-ons like "She was a tremendous control freak whose refusal to allow me to make my judgments made me want to go down the hall screaming obscenities"—even though that may be the most honest answer.

The key to learning this method is to maintain your tone authentic so that even if your comments are brief, they don't come out as harsh or dismissive. It's more about sticking to one primary issue in every question instead of going into a nervous tangent. And don't worry—if the interviewer wants you to elaborate on a given topic, she'll ask.

5. Think Positively

Finally, soothe your anxiety by convincing yourself that you deserve to be there. Hey, you wouldn't have been invited to interview if you weren't being seriously considered as a candidate! Use this knowledge to your advantage to mentally build yourself up before the interview. It can take the edge off sufficiently to allow you to approach the issue with a burst of self-assurance and confidence.

Most importantly, remember that while you need to be calm, composed, and confident to score the job, an interview is not a life-or-death situation. Hiring managers are humans, too—and they'll understand and forgive a few little nervous blips.

CHAPTER SEVEN; TIPS FOR CONTRACT ROLE INTERVIEWS

If you've been in your current contracting work for some time, you might be out of touch with contemporary interviewing tactics and a bit rusty sitting in front of an interviewer. Find below a complete candidate checklist that teaches you how to prepare, what questions to expect and how to conduct yourself during the interview.

How to prepare for a contractor interview
There's a lot to think about before an interview, so here's how to get up to speed:

Find out about the firm

Before your interview, you should find out the following about the company:
What are its products or service?
How big is the company?
Who are its competitors?

Aside from the information your agency may supply, you should perform your research from corporate literature, web searches, and word of mouth, if possible.

Find out what structure the interview will follow
Pick out your abilities or achievements that are directly relevant and rehearse these ahead of the interview. Find opportunities to market yourself, tying your expertise to the career you are seeking for.

Most interviews follow a similar format:

Questions based on your CV to clarify your work path and aspirations
Rehearse abilities and achievements that are directly relevant;
Be prepared to explain any atypical portions of your CV, such as any significant periods taken out for education or traveling instances including:

How much do you know about this position?
What intrigues you about the job?
What experience or skills do you have that make you suited for this job?
Tell me about/why did you leave your last contract?
What intrigues you about this company?
When have you had the opportunity to display initiative?
Who and what were you responsible for at your last job?
Give an example of when you coped successfully under pressure.

Do you prefer to work as an individual or as part of a team?
What are your three biggest achievements so far in your career?
What do you regard as your strengths and weaknesses?
What are your long-term goals? How are you going to succeed in accomplishing them?
Are you considering any other roles?

CHAPTER Eight: INTERVIEW CONCLUSION TECHNIQUES

Finishing a job interview on a good note is vital in boosting your chances of receiving an offer. The closing statement you deliver can help you make a lasting impression on the hiring manager and separate you from other candidates.

What are closing statements?
A closing statement explains why you're the right candidate for the position that you're interviewing for. The statement highlights how your abilities and work experience may assist the organization.

Why are closing statements important?

Here are a few reasons why a closing statement is important:

Expresses your interest in collaborating with the company: The closing sentence displays your eagerness about the position. Discuss a few main reasons why this role is the right fit for you and the organization.

Underscores your talents and qualifications: A closing remark reveals how successfully you promote yourself to an employer. Give two or three examples of how well your abilities and experiences can assist the organization to prosper if they elect to hire you.

Answers questions by the employer: An employer may ask follow-up questions at the end of the interview to discover more about a past job you held or a talent you've learned. The quality of your concluding speech can could their questions before they ask them.

10 types of closing speeches for interviews

Depending on your inclination, you can use your concluding remark to transmit extra information or ask critical questions.

You might utilize your interview concluding statement to:

1. Ask important questions

One technique you could impress the hiring manager is to give insightful questions that suggest you've done your research and that you've been actively listening throughout the interview. It also reaffirms your interest in the role. Some types of questions you could ask are:

"How does your company outsell competitors within your industry?"
"Do you require me to work in other areas of the organization to produce results?"
"What measures does the corporation do to improve the organization's culture?"

"What types of professional development opportunities does the company offer?"

"2. Discuss the missing experience

Addressing missing experience to a hiring manager displays how you can achieve despite challenges. The recruiting manager can notice your problem-solving talents and weigh them into their choice to hire you. Here are two closing statements you can make:

"I appreciate your concerns about my experience. Despite the minimal expertise I have with project management software, I acquired more about them when I recognized this as a necessary talent in the job description. I feel that I can master this new program swiftly to enhance productivity in this function

"I do not have past knowledge of selling marketing services, but I think my ability to increase my customer base by 30% at my current position makes me a suitable contender for this work. You must discover the greatest techniques to explore and assimilate understanding about fresh products before you market them."

3. Remind the recruiting manager of your most crucial skills

Finish your final argument by stressing your strongest skills. Sometimes you might have to remind them about what you've learned. You need to describe how you can employ these qualities to the task and how it can make a favorable effect on the rest of the team. Review this closing statement:

"My time management and problem-solving skills qualify me for the human resources assistant post. When I interned for an entertainment company, I took responsibility for producing presentations for executives along with organizing meetings with prominent artists in the music industry. I raised the department's completion of duties by 15% during my tenure there, and I think I can elevate my performance at this organization."

4. Emphasize your love for the position

Employers want to find out if you're committed to working in a position. Keep these comments short and talk about what you love about the firm and job responsibilities. You can use something like this.

"This employment is a win-win for me because I've wanted to work in the medical field since fourth grade. Working with patients is my favorite component of this job, and it's an opportunity to strengthen my interpersonal skills."

5. Speak about the next steps

Asking about the next steps indicates your interest in the position to the interviewer. It might reflect how confident you are to thrive in this role. Here are various techniques to query about the next steps:

"Do you know when I can hear about the subsequent steps of the hiring process?"
"When are you looking to fill in this position?
\s
"\ When are you contacting candidates regarding the subsequent steps?"

6. Determine if the employer needs more information
Asking an employer for additional information presents you with another chance to demonstrate your talents. Bring a copy of your CV and portfolio if you think it applies to the role. Here are some questions you may ask:

"Do you need any information about my candidacy? I have a copy of my portfolio and case studies of former clients I've worked with if you're interested."
"I have created several relationships since commencing my work in finance. Do you need to see a copy of my references?"
"Does the rest of the leadership team require copies of my resume?"

7. Finish with a courteous conclusion
A great ending offers a positive image to the hiring manager, and it describes how you handle yourself in a professional environment. Here are some frequent conclusions:

"I am grateful for interviewing with you today. You have provided me with a good understanding of the situation. I think my experience and accomplishments can add value to the organization. Is there anything more you need to clarify if I am the appropriate contender for this position?"

"Thank you for making time to interview me for the available role. I am pleased about the notion of working in this job and being a part of a highly renowned team."

8. Ask for the job directly

Asking for a job is brave, but an employer can appreciate your confidence. You should have a backup reaction in case they say no straight away, but it does not prohibit you from receiving the job. Here is a strategy to ask for a job and a response if they decline to grant you an offer:

"I understand why you need time to explore other prospects. I'm excited to hear from you about your decision. Do you have a timeframe of when you'll contact candidates?"

9. Offer a good perspective for the firm

Discuss the future of the company with you as an employee. Gather insight from research about the organization and from questions you ask about challenges they're seeking solutions on.

10. Show how you're prepared for your first day

Convey your plan and method to improve the organization. Employers will pay attention to the minutiae of your plan, but they'll also adore your passion and devotion.

CHAPTER NINE: THE POWER OF FOLLOWING UP.

Finishing a job interview on a favorable note is crucial in enhancing your chances of receiving an offer. The closing statement you provide can help you make a lasting impression on the hiring manager and separate you from other candidates.

What are closing statements?
A closing statement shows why you're the right applicant for the position that you're interviewing for. The statement illustrates how your abilities and work experience may aid the organization.

Why are closing statements important?

Here are a few reasons why a closing remark is important:

Expresses your interest in cooperating with the company: The concluding sentence reflects your eagerness for the position. Discuss a few primary reasons why this role is the best fit for you and the organization.

Underscores your talents and qualifications: A final statement reflects how successfully you offer yourself to an employer. Give two or three examples of how well your abilities and experiences can assist the organization to prosper if they chose to hire you.

Answers inquiries by the employer: An employer may ask follow-up questions at the end of the interview to discover more about a former job you held or a talent you've learned. The quality of your conclusion speech can could their questions before they ask them.

10 types of closing speeches for interviews

Depending on your preference, you can use your final remark to relay further information or ask important questions.

You may apply your interview conclusion statement to:

1. Ask important questions

One approach you could impress the hiring manager is to give intelligent questions that imply you've done your study and that you've been actively listening throughout the interview. It also reaffirms your interest in the role. Some types of questions you could ask are:

"How does your company outsell competitors within your industry?"
"Do you require me to work in other areas of the organization to accomplish results?"
"What measures does the corporation do to improve the organization's culture?"
"What types of professional development opportunities does the company offer?"

"2. Discuss the missing experience

Addressing missing experience to a hiring manager illustrates how you can succeed despite challenges. The recruiting manager can notice your problem-solving talents and weigh them into their choice to hire you. Here are two closing statements you can make:

"I appreciate your concerns about my experience. Despite the small skill I have with project management software, I acquired more about them when I recognized this as a vital talent in the job description. I feel that I can master this new program rapidly to boost productivity in this function

"I do not have past knowledge of selling marketing services, but I think my capacity to build my customer base by 30% in my current position makes me a suitable candidate for this employment. You must discover the ideal approaches to study and assimilate information about fresh products before you advertise them."

3. Remind the hiring manager of your most critical skills

Finish your final argument by emphasizing your finest skills. Sometimes you might have to remind them about what you've learned. You need to describe how you can use these characteristics in the assignment and how they can produce a good effect on the rest of the team. Review this closing statement:

"My time management and problem-solving skills qualify me for the human resources assistant post. When I interned for an entertainment company, I took responsibility for making presentations for executives along with coordinating meetings with major musicians in the music industry. I boosted the department's completion of duties by 15% throughout my employment there, and I think I can elevate my performance at this organization."

4. Emphasize your love for the role

Employers want to find out if you're committed to working in a position. Keep your comments short and talk about what you enjoy about the firm and your job responsibilities. You can use something like this.

"This position is a win-win for me because I've wanted to work in the medical industry since fourth grade. Working with patients is my favorite component of this work, and it's an opportunity to enhance my interpersonal skills."

5. Speak about the next steps

Asking about the next steps signals your interest in the position to the interviewer. It can represent how sure you are to thrive in your role. Here are numerous approaches to question the following steps:

"Do you know when I can hear about the remaining steps of the hiring process?"
"When are you looking to fill in this position?
\s\s"\sWhen are you contacting candidates regarding the upcoming steps?"

6. Determine if the employer needs more information

Asking an employer for additional information offers you another chance to demonstrate your talents. Bring a copy of your CV and portfolio if you think it applies to the post. Here are some questions you may ask:

"Do you need any information about my candidacy? I have a copy of my portfolio and case studies of prior clients I've worked with if you're interested."

"I have made various relationships since started my profession in finance. Do you need to see a copy of my references?"

"Does the rest of the leadership team require copies of my resume?"

7. Finish with a courteous conclusion

A fantastic finish presents a nice image to the hiring manager, and it describes how you treat yourself in a professional context. Here are some frequent conclusions:

"I am grateful for interviewing with you today. You have provided me with a thorough knowledge of the situation. I think my experience and accomplishments can add value to the organization. Is there anything more you need to clarify if I am the ideal competitor for this position?"
"Thank you for making time to interview me for the open post. I am excited about the thought of working in this career and becoming a part of a highly famous team."

8. Ask for the job directly
Asking for a job is brave, but an employer can appreciate your confidence. You should have a backup reaction in case they say no straight away, but it does not stop you from receiving the job. Here is a technique to ask for a job and a response if they deny to provide you an offer:

"I understand why you need time to examine alternative prospects. I'm excited to hear from you about your decision. Do you have a timeframe of when you'll contact candidates?"

9. Offer a strong perspective for the firm
Discuss the future of the company with you as an employee. Gather insight from research about the organization and from questions you ask about difficulties they're seeking solutions on.

10. Show how you're prepared for your first day
Convey your plan and method to improve the organization. Employers will pay attention to the intricacy of your plan, but they'll also appreciate your passion and devotion.

CHAPTER TEN: YOU HAVE BEEN HIRED!! CAREER MANAGEMENT TIPS.

Before you accept that job offer or even provide a verbal commitment, there are a few measures that you'll need to take to set yourself up for success. To guarantee you're making the best moves after the offer, we're breaking it all down for you. So read on. And—oh yeah—congrats!

1. Be Ready for the Call

When HR calls with a job offer, you might be inclined to give a fast reaction. The idea here is to have a sentence ready to go, such as, "Thank you so much for the offer. I am excited about this opportunity. When would you like a response by?"

By utilizing non-committal language like the one above, you'll demonstrate your eagerness for the task, while also giving yourself time to make a well-informed decision.

Most organizations will be more than eager to give you time to evaluate information and consider the offer. If an employer requires an immediate decision, that's a red flag. Consider long and hard if this is a company you want to work for.

2. Review the Written Offer

Around this time, you should be receiving a written offer letter from HR. This is your opportunity to analyze the offer amount, as well as if included, perks, benefits, time off, and sign-on incentives.

To find out if the income given is in line with market standards, examine sites like Payscale or Glassdoor.

When assessing if your income is on par, take a hard look at each perk, making sure to evaluate them all against one other. For example, if your income is somewhat below the industry norm but the vacation time is overly gracious, then maybe you don't need to seek a rise.

3. Negotiate a Counter Offer

If the offer is below what you expected after considering all of the other business benefits, you might seek to negotiate a more fitting wage.

Now's the time to draft a counteroffer letter.

Beginning your letter with a statement of interest and enthusiasm for the job, including your key-selling points such as how you aim to contribute to the firm. Following that, compose your counter offer, a wage that should be justified via your study on the market and/or the added value you propose to bring to the organization.

Be ready for the corporation to come back, either way, rejecting or accepting your counteroffer.

Whatever the outcome, demonstrate your gratitude, and leave the conversation on a nice note.

4. Let Other Potential Employers Know

In case you were also interviewing with other organizations, you'll need to advise them you've accepted another job offer. A simple email will do. State to them anything along the lines of:

I wanted to convey my heartfelt appreciation for your considering me as a candidate for the [position name] post. I liked meeting your staff and learning more about the outstanding work you perform.

I am writing to respectfully withdraw myself from consideration since I was given another employment that more closely corresponds with my skill set and ambitions.

I wish the best for everyone at [business name] and hope that, in the future, we have another chance to work together.

Thank you again for this chance.

Sincerely,

[Your Name]

5. Send a Thank You Email

After accepting the job offer, it's a fantastic idea to send a quick thank you note to your new employer and HR contact. Not only does this help to express your excitement for the position, but also works to keep you on faultless terms with the organization as they finalize your paperwork.

Keep this letter simple. Something like this would work great:

I wanted to properly thank you for the job offer at [Company Name]. I am extremely excited to begin working, learning more about the organization, and finding opportunities to apply my expertise to the team.

Please reach out at any moment if you need anything else from me. The best way to contact me is by email, but feel free to call me as well at [number].

Again, thank you for this chance. I can't wait to begin working for such a fantastic team.

Sincerely,

[Your Name]

6. Don't Update Your Online Job Status—Yet\sSure, you're delighted to update your LinkedIn and other social networks with your newly minted job title. But it's better to wait.

Once you've been with your employer for a few months and are convinced it's the place for you, then it's a safe time to update your social networks with your new job title.

CONCLUSION

If you have gotten to this point, I can assure you that you have got all it takes to ace that interview and secure your dream job
I suggest you start by identifying where you are in this journey and take off while converting all your wrongs to right.

GOOD LUCK AS YOU GO GET THAT JOB!

www.ingramcontent.com/pod-product-compliance
Lightning Source LLC
LaVergne TN
LVHW050335160826
845677LV00014B/3620

* 9 7 9 8 3 5 3 3 4 3 1 7 2 *